A Little Girl After God's Own Heart

Elizabeth George

paintings by *Judy Luenebrink*

HARVEST HOUSE PUBLISHERS

EUGENE, OREGON

A LITTLE GIRL AFTER GOD'S OWN HEART

Text copyright © 2006 by Elizabeth George
Artwork copyright © 2006 by Judy Luenebrink
Published by Harvest House Publishers
Eugene, Oregon 97402

ISBN-13: 978-0-7369-1545-8
ISBN-10: 0-7369-1545-1

Cover by Harvest House Publishers, Katie Brady designer

Scripture quotations are from *The International Children's Bible*, New Century Version, copyright © 1986 by Word Publishing, Nashville, Tennessee. Used by permission.

Printed in the United States of America

08 09 10 11 12 13 14 / LT / 10 9 8 7 6 5 4

Elizabeth George
P.O. Box 2879
Belfair, WA 98528
1-800-542-4611
www.elizabethgeorge.com

Judy Luenebrink
1-818-888-9934
www.judyluenebrink.com

These verses and this book are written for you, our cherished granddaughters.
May you always follow after God's heart.

Dear friend,

    There is nothing quite as special as a little girl! And there's nothing as rewarding as helping that little girl to blossom and grow in character. In this book you'll find nine qualities that are important for the little girls in your life to know about, and to nurture in their daily lives. Every child struggles with being nice, staying calm, extending kindness, and showing love. But God makes His help and instruction available.

    So gather up your little girls and come along. Read about some of the everyday decisions little ones must make. Introduce them to the unchanging scriptures that teach them the right things to do and the right choices to make. Let them see how God's way is always the best way! You'll be delighted as you witness the seed you are planting into precious little hearts begin to bear fruit.

    In His everlasting love,

Elizabeth George

A Heart Filled with...

Love

"Love each other,
because love comes from God."

1 JOHN 4:7

Love

"God is love" and wants love from you,
To show forth His heart in all that you do.
So don't be so selfish and stop being stingy.
Be more like God—as much as you can be!

Hmmm...
How many toys can I share today?
How many smiles to those on my way?
How many kind deeds for those who are blue?
God, help me give love in the ways that You do.

A Heart Filled with...

Joy
and
Peace

"Be full of joy and
live in peace with each other."

PHILIPPIANS 4:4 and 1 THESSALONIANS 5:13

Joy and Peace

You can have joy and peace all day long—
When all is good...or if everything's wrong!
A girl after God is one who knows
Her heart's the place where happiness grows.

You can share peace and joy with others,
With Mom and Dad, sisters and brothers.
When their days crash in and get out of whack,
Be sure to give them a nice pat on the back.

"Be patient with every person."

1 Thessalonians 5:14

Patience

What can you do when there's a delay,
When things take forever, seems like all day?
You can get red-hot mad and throw a huge fit,
Or you can be patient and quietly sit.

God's girl can wait...for hours in a row,
Till things start to happen, till it's time to go.
She tries to do nothing she'll later regret,
To calm herself down and not get upset.

A Heart Filled with...

Kindness
and
Goodness

"Be kind and do good to people who need help."

PROVERBS 3:27 AND EPHESIANS 4:32

Kindness and Goodness

Oh, to be kind and to always do good,
To say words that help and do what you should!
To quit being mean and making folks sad,
To be really sweet so they will be glad.

Lord, help me bring cheer to those who are down,
To kids who are troubled and wearing a frown.
Let me share comfort, show mercy, and serve,
And give more to others than they may deserve.

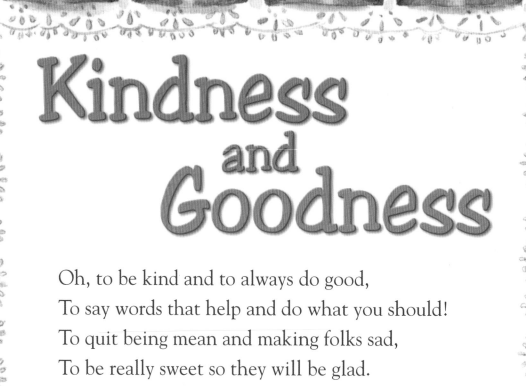

A Heart Filled with...

Faithfulness

"It is hard to find someone who
really can be trusted."

PROVERBS 20:6

Faithfulness

Has a friend ever hurt you who wanted to play,
And you couldn't wait for that red-letter day?
She said she'd come over—rain, sleet, or snow,
But when the time came, she didn't show.

God says that you're to be faithful and true,
That people should know they can count upon you.
Let your yes be yes, and your no be no.
If you say you'll be there, be sure that you go.

A Heart Filled with...

Gentleness

"Be gentle and polite to all people."

TITUS 3:2

Gentleness

A gal who is gentle in heart knows full well,
When things fall apart not to stomp, scream, or yell.
A girl after God is all sugar and spice.
She speaks words with care and does what is nice.

When things go wrong, just take a step back—
Calm down, be thoughtful, and please, don't attack!
Don't be ugly or awful or look for a fight,
Don't be hateful or bossy, but gentle and quiet.

A Heart Filled with...

Self-Control

"Never shout angrily or say things to hurt others. Never do anything evil."

EPHESIANS 4:31

Self-Control

Why's it so hard to do what is right?
To hold myself in instead of ignite?
God wants His kids to say "No!" to what's bad,
To be in control instead of get mad.

Dear Father above, please help me to be
The sweet little girl You so want to see—
A gal full of goodness, loving and true,
Who's wanting to grow to be more like You.

Words to Know

Stingy: doesn't like to share

Deeds: acts of kindness

Blue: sad

Delay: wait, slow down

Regret: be sorry for

Mercy: showing kindness to others

Red-letter day: a very special day

Self-control: calm, even-tempered

Ignite: get angry